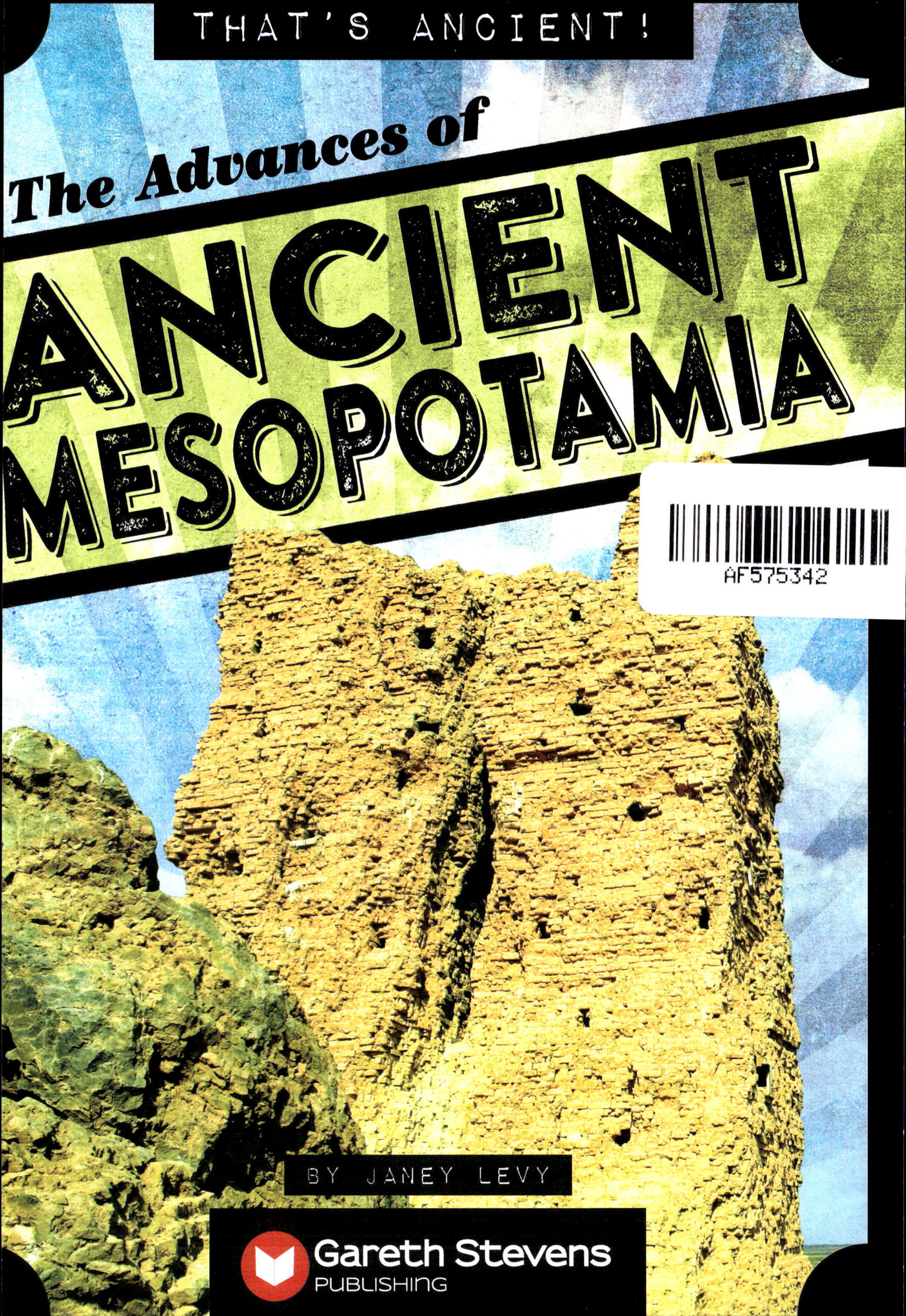

THAT'S ANCIENT!

The Advances of ANCIENT MESOPOTAMIA

BY JANEY LEVY

Gareth Stevens PUBLISHING

Please visit our website, www.garethstevens.com. For a free color catalog of all our high-quality books, call toll free 1-800-542-2595 or fax 1-877-542-2596.

Library of Congress Cataloging-in-Publication Data

Names: Levy, Janey, author. | Levy, Janey. That's ancient!
Title: The advances of ancient Mesopotamia / Janey Levy.
Description: New York : Gareth Stevens Publishing, [2022] | Series: That's ancient! | Includes bibliographical references and index.
Identifiers: LCCN 2020042190 (print) | LCCN 2020042191 (ebook) | ISBN 9781538265635 (library binding) | ISBN 9781538265611 (paperback) | ISBN 9781538265628 (set) | ISBN 9781538265642 (ebook)
Subjects: LCSH: Iraq—History—To 634—Juvenile literature. | Iraq—Civilization—To 634—Juvenile literature.
Classification: LCC DS71 .L53 2022 (print) | LCC DS71 (ebook) | DDC 935—dc23
LC record available at https://lccn.loc.gov/2020042190
LC ebook record available at https://lccn.loc.gov/2020042191

First Edition

Published in 2022 by
Gareth Stevens Publishing
29 E. 21st Street
New York, NY 10010

Designer: Katelyn E. Reynolds
Editor: Therese Shea

Photo credits: Cover, pp. 1, 12 Homo Cosmicos/Shutterstock.com; cover, pp. 1–32 (burst) Dawid Lech/Shutterstock.com; cover, pp. 1–32 (clouds) javarman/Shutterstock.com; p. 5 Porcupen/Shutterstock.com; p. 7 SSPL/Getty Images; pp. 9, 13 (bottom) Essam Al-Sudani/AFP via Getty Images; p. 11 (cylinder seal) Marie-Lan Nguyen (2006)/Jastrow/Wikipedia.org; p. 11 (*Ram in a Thicket*) Benjamin82877/Wikipedia.org; p. 11 (small stone figure) Fletcher Fund, 1940/Metropolitan Museum of Art/Pharos/Wikipedia.org; pp. 11 (*Victory Stele of Naram-Sin*), 28 Louvre Museum/Rama/Wikipedia.org; p. 13 (top) Asaad Niazi/AFP via Getty Images; p. 15 (top) Egoreichenkov Evgenii/Shutterstock.com; p. 15 (bottom) Universal History Archive/Universal Images Group via Getty Images; p. 17 Marie-Lan Nguyen/Louvre Museum/Jastrow/Wikipedia.org; pp. 17 (*Epic of Gilgamesh*), 27 Osama Shukir Muhammed Amin FRCP(Glasg)/Neuroforever/Wikipedia.org; p. 19 Josell7/Wikipedia.org; p. 21 (clock) Photoongraphy/Shutterstock.com; p. 21 Mike Pellinni/Shutterstock.com; p. 23 Zvereva Yana/Shutterstock.com; p. 25 CM Dixon/Print Collector/Getty Images.

Printed in the United States of America

CPSIA compliance information: Batch #CWGS22: For further information, contact Gareth Stevens, New York, New York, at 1-800-542-2595.

CONTENTS

Ancient Mesopotamia 4
No Longer Hunter-Gatherers 6
Settlement to City 8
Art and Architecture 10
Round and Round 14
Write That Down 16
You Can Count on It 18
The Invention of Time 20
Charting the Sky 22
On the Wind 24
Medicine Beyond Magic 26
The Cradle of Civilization 28
Glossary 30
For More Information 31
Index 32

Words in the glossary appear in **bold** type the first time they are used in the text.

Ancient Mesopotamia

Have you ever heard of Mesopotamia (meh-suh-puh-TAY-mee-uh)? That's the name given to the ancient region in southwestern Asia where the world's earliest civilizations arose. The name itself comes from Greek words meaning "between the rivers." These rivers are the Tigris (TY-gruhs) and the Euphrates (yoo-FRAY-teez). No land called Mesopotamia exists today. The area it covered now corresponds roughly to modern-day Iraq, as well as parts of today's Iran, Syria, Kuwait, and Turkey.

So what makes Mesopotamia special? It's where cities first arose. It's where the wheel was invented. It's where writing originated. And those are just a few of the accomplishments of Mesopotamian civilizations. Read on to learn much more about the amazing achievements of ancient Mesopotamia.

THAT'S FASCINATING!

Mesopotamia is known by several other names. It's also called the Fertile **Crescent** and the Cradle of Civilization.

MESOPOTAMIA

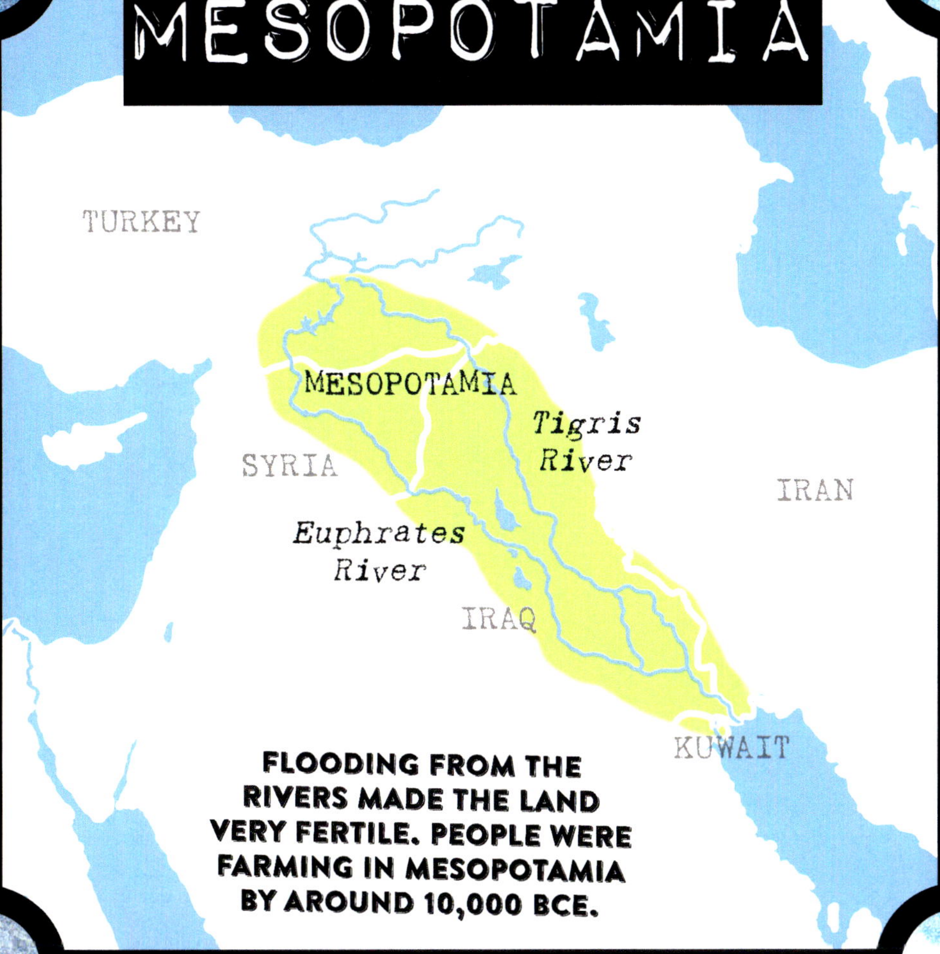

FLOODING FROM THE RIVERS MADE THE LAND VERY FERTILE. PEOPLE WERE FARMING IN MESOPOTAMIA BY AROUND 10,000 BCE.

Many Civilizations

It's a mistake to think of Mesopotamia as being something like a country with just a single civilization. In fact, civilizations arose there long, long before anything like modern nations existed. The area was home to many different civilizations. These civilizations existed side by side, and they changed over time. Mesopotamian civilizations included the Sumerians, the Akkadians, the Babylonians, and the Assyrians, all of whom made significant contributions to history.

NO LONGER HUNTER-GATHERERS

Agriculture is a normal part of modern life. It supplies the food we buy at the store. But it hasn't always existed. You can thank Mesopotamians for its invention.

Once, Mesopotamians were hunter-gatherers. Do you know the term "hunter-gatherer"? It refers to people who get their food by hunting animals and gathering wild plants. Hunter-gatherers live a **nomadic** life, and nomadic life in Mesopotamia was hard. Resources were scarce, and that led to fighting.

Then, Mesopotamians began to grow crops such as wheat, barley, and peas. They invented the plow and, along with Egypt, irrigation systems. They also began to raise animals such as cattle, goats, sheep, and pigs. This was the invention of agriculture, and it changed life. People could settle down and live in one place. Small communities emerged.

THAT'S FASCINATING!

Changes in climate helped make the shift to a settled farming lifestyle possible. After millions of years of cold temperatures, temperatures began to rise, which made it easier for Mesopotamians to grow crops.

THIS MODEL SHOWS WHAT A MESOPOTAMIAN HOUSE MIGHT HAVE LOOKED LIKE AROUND 5000 BCE. HOUSES WERE BUILT OF BRICKS MADE OF CLAY AND STRAW. THE BRICKS WERE SHAPED AND DRIED IN THE SUN BEFORE BEING USED TO BUILD. THE ROOF WAS LIKELY MADE OF BRANCHES AND MUD.

Jarmo

The settlement called Jarmo, established around 6750 BCE, was the earliest agricultural community in Mesopotamia. It had about 20 to 25 square, mud-brick houses, each of which had several rooms. Evidence shows the people grew wheat and barley, and had the equipment to grind grain. They raised goats, sheep, and pigs but still hunted. They had ovens made of mud, bone spoons, and bone needles for sewing.

Settlement TO CITY

Perhaps you live in a city or have visited one. They're big, often exciting places. But after what you've read, you probably realize cities haven't always existed. Hunter-gatherers definitely didn't live in them. And the settlement of Jarmo, with no more than 25 houses, certainly couldn't be called a city. However, the growth of farming that led to settlements eventually led to the rise of the first cities.

Eridu, established between about 5000 BCE and 4000 BCE, was one of the oldest cities. An ancient Mesopotamian myth says Eridu was the first city in the world, created by the gods. Archaeologists aren't sure it's the oldest, though. The ancient city of Uruk was founded around the same time—or perhaps even a little earlier. About 1,500 years later, Mesopotamia had around 40 cities.

THAT'S FASCINATING!

At one point, Uruk may have been home to 50,000 people! That's amazing, especially when you consider that the first agricultural settlement in the region had only 20 to 25 houses.

THIS IS WHAT REMAINS TODAY OF THE ANCIENT CITY OF URUK.

City-States

Out of Mesopotamian cities grew city-states. Each of these consisted of a city—or sometimes several cities—and its surrounding territory. That territory would include smaller towns and villages as well as farm fields. Each city-state was protected by its own god, and there was a temple to that god in the central city. City-states were independent, but sometimes they formed leagues with one another. These leagues might have been for trade, mutual protection, or working together on large projects.

ART AND ARCHITECTURE

The rise of agriculture and cities changed society. Not everyone needed to hunt or farm in order to have enough food. Specialized trades developed, including art.

Much of Mesopotamian art focused on two important aspects of society: religion and honoring the ruler. Small stone figures of people standing with hands clasped in front of them were temple offerings to a god. The piece of art called the *Victory* ***Stele*** *of Naram-Sin* celebrates Mesopotamian king Naram-Sin—the large figure at the top—leading his soldiers to victory in battle.

Costly materials were used in objects made for royalty, as in the piece *Ram in the Thicket*. Found in the royal tombs of the ancient city of Ur, it was made of gold, silver, and a blue stone called lapis lazuli.

THAT'S FASCINATING!

Much of early Mesopotamian art was small, but later Mesopotamian art was sometimes **monumental**. For example, a figure of a human-headed winged bull that once stood beside a palace doorway was nearly 14 feet (4.3 m) tall!

RAM IN THE THICKET

SMALL STONE FIGURE, TEMPLE OFFERING

VICTORY STELE OF NARAM-SIN

THESE ARE JUST A FEW EXAMPLES OF REMARKABLE MESOPOTAMIAN ART.

The Cylinder Seal

The cylinder seal may seem like a strange concept to modern people, but it was a common—even necessary—art form in Mesopotamia. It was a small, carved stone or metal tube used as a stamp. The seal's carving told the owner's story, and it was rolled in the moist clay on which documents were written to serve as the owner's signature. Everyone had a seal, including enslaved people, and people carried their seal with them on a string or pinned to their clothing.

Monumental **architecture** also emerged in Mesopotamian cities. It took the form of a huge structure built in the city center to support a temple that honored the city's patron, or protector, god. The structure was called a ziggurat (ZIH-guh-rat). The ziggurat first appeared in the city of Uruk and then spread throughout Mesopotamia from there.

The ziggurat was a pyramid-like structure. But instead of having smooth, sloping sides, the sides were like giant steps. The top was flat instead of pointed, and on the top was the temple. Stairs on the outside of the structure led to the temple at the top. The inner part of a ziggurat was built of plain mud brick. The outer part was covered with oven-baked, painted mud brick.

DRAWING OF THE ZIGGURAT IN THE CITY OF UR

A Lost Secret

Concrete is an important building material in the modern world. Ancient Romans are usually credited with inventing it, but it seems Mesopotamians came close. Around 3000 BCE, the people of the city of Uruk were using an artificial stone that was an ancestor of concrete. Unfortunately, the secret of how to make it has been lost. But other evidence of artificial stone exists. An artificial form of basalt, a volcanic stone, was discovered in a Mesopotamian city that existed over 1,000 years later.

BECAUSE ZIGGURATS WERE BUILT OF MUD BRICK, NONE HAVE SURVIVED COMPLETE.

THAT'S FASCINATING!

The sloping sides and steps of the ziggurats were often planted with trees and shrubs so that they looked like gardens.

Round and ROUND

Today, people rely a lot on wheels for **transportation**. Cars, buses, trains, and bicycles all use wheels. But would you believe all those wheels owe their existence to a device created for a specialized trade that emerged in ancient Mesopotamian cities? That device was the potter's wheel.

Pottery had existed in Mesopotamia for thousands of years. It was made by hand, with the potter moving around the piece to shape it. By 3500 BCE, the potter's wheel had been invented. The potter put clay on the wheel and turned the wheel to shape it rather than having to move around it. Potters could produce pieces faster and thus produce more pieces.

About 300 years later, it dawned on someone that wheels could have another use. That's when **chariots** were invented.

THAT'S FASCINATING!

Not everyone in Mesopotamia had a chariot. Chariots were transportation for royalty and the wealthy only.

HERE YOU CAN SEE A POTTER'S WHEEL AT WORK, AS WELL AS MESOPOTAMIAN ARTWORK FROM ABOUT 2500 BCE SHOWING A CHARIOT.

An Amazing Discovery

In 1922, the archaeologist Leonard Woolley was excavating at the site where the ancient city of Ur once stood. He uncovered the royal tombs there, and in them he found what remained of two chariots. These were the oldest wheeled **vehicles** ever found! He found their tires too. You might think the tires would be made of rubber, like modern tires, but rubber was unknown in Mesopotamia. Their tires were made of leather.

Write That DOWN

You probably write every day, either using a computer or smartphone or on paper. But humans got along without writing for thousands of years. The need for writing arose after people began living in cities. Writing was invented in Mesopotamia around 3500 BCE.

Once people started living in cities, they began trading with other cities for goods they needed but didn't have. Trade required written communication and record keeping. The earliest writing was pictographic, which means pictures represented objects.

Eventually, a new form of writing developed in which symbols represented sounds instead of objects. This new writing system, invented in the city of Uruk, is called cuneiform (kyoo-NEE-uh-form). Cuneiform gets its name from the Latin word *cuneus*, which means "wedge." That's because the symbols look wedge-like.

THAT'S FASCINATING!

Mesopotamians didn't have pens, pencils, or paper. They used a writing tool made of reed called a stylus to make wedge-like marks on wet clay, which was then dried.

THIS CUNEIFORM DOCUMENT IS A CONTRACT FOR THE SALE OF A HOUSE AND A FIELD.

The Epic of Gilgamesh

Cuneiform was used to write ***The Epic of Gilgamesh*** around 2150 BCE. It was the first epic poem in the world and is among the oldest existing works of literature. It tells the story of the ancient king of Uruk. After the death of a friend, Gilgamesh goes on a quest to find the meaning of life and to defeat death. He fails to conquer death, but he wins a kind of immortality by writing down his story.

You Can COUNT ON IT

Trade between ancient Mesopotamian cities required more than writing. It required precise counting of goods sent and received. This is how early Mesopotamians became the first people to develop the concept of counting. Think about that. Can you imagine a time when the very idea of counting didn't exist? It was this development that eventually gave birth to mathematics.

Early Mesopotamians also developed the concept of place value. Place value is fundamental to the modern number system as well, so you're familiar with it. It means the position, or place, of a digit within a number determines its value. In the modern base 10 system, each place represents 10 times the value of the place to its right. Mesopotamians used a base 60, or sexagesimal (sehk-suh-JEH-suh-muhl), system!

THAT'S FASCINATING!

Cuneiform numerals are among the symbols that appear on the very earliest written documents.

THIS CHART SHOWS HOW MESOPOTAMIANS WROTE NUMBERS 1 THROUGH 59 IN CUNEIFORM.

1	11	21	31	41	51
2	12	22	32	42	52
3	13	23	33	43	53
4	14	24	34	44	54
5	15	25	35	45	55
6	16	26	36	46	56
7	17	27	37	47	57
8	18	28	38	48	58
9	19	29	39	49	59
10	20	30	40	50	

The Invention of Nothing

The difference between 22 and 2,020 is enormous. What tells us the difference between them in our place-value system is the zeros. In the number 2,020, zeros are placeholders in the ones and hundreds places. Although there are no ones or hundreds, the zeros occupy those places to tell us the values of the twos. Thus, the zeros are extremely important. And zero—as a placeholder—was invented by Mesopotamians.

The Invention OF TIME

Have you ever wondered why an hour has 60 minutes and a minute has 60 seconds? Think about our base 10 math system for a moment. It influences things like our money system. A dime equals 10 pennies. A dollar equals 10 dimes or 100 pennies. So why doesn't an hour have 100 minutes and a minute have 100 seconds? You can thank the Mesopotamians for that.

The Mesopotamians were the first to measure time and divide it into units. That is, they created hours and minutes. When they divided time into hours and minutes, they naturally relied on their base 60 math system. They gave each hour 60 minutes and each minute 60 seconds. The system they established has survived to this day.

THAT'S FASCINATING!

Mesopotamians also created the 24-hour day. They divided the day into two periods: a 12-hour period for daylight and a 12-hour period for night.

WHENEVER YOU LOOK AT A CLOCK NOW, YOU SHOULD THINK OF THE MESOPOTAMIANS AND THEIR CONCEPT OF TIME!

Why Base 60?

Why did the Mesopotamians use a base 60 math system? The theory points to ancient counting practices. Many ancient civilizations counted to 12 by counting the three sections of each finger on one hand (not including the thumb). In fact, 12 was an important number to the Mesopotamians. Some experts think 60 came about by multiplying the three sections of each finger on one hand (12) by all five fingers of the other hand (5). However, no one is sure.

Charting THE SKY

You probably use a calendar often to determine such things as when an assignment is due or when you're going to the dentist. But have you ever wondered who invented the calendar? You can thank Mesopotamians for that.

Mesopotamians invented the first calendar. To do this, they charted the celestial movements of the sun, moon, and stars. They also charted the movements of the five planets visible to the naked, or unaided, eye. Those planets are Mercury, Venus, Mars, Jupiter, and Saturn. They couldn't see additional planets because the telescope hadn't been invented yet. Mesopotamians used the knowledge they gained in creating the calendar to determine the best times for planting and harvesting crops. They were also able to forecast events such as eclipses.

THAT'S FASCINATING!

Since Mesopotamians believed celestial bodies moved according to the gods' will, they interpreted certain astronomical events as messages from the gods. This led to astrology, which is the study of celestial bodies' effects on human beings.

MESOPOTAMIANS INTERPRETED THE MOVEMENTS THEY CHARTED IN THE SKY AS BEING DIRECTED BY THE WILL OF THE GODS, JUST LIKE EVERYTHING ELSE IN THE UNIVERSE.

What's Your Sign?

Have you ever read your daily **horoscope**? Many people do. Your horoscope is based on the idea that what happens to you is determined by your **zodiac** sign. Would you be surprised to learn Mesopotamians invented horoscopes—as well as astrology and the zodiac? And while you might read your horoscope for fun, Mesopotamians were quite serious about horoscopes and astrology. They sincerely believed a person's zodiac sign determined their character and fate.

On the WIND

You've read that trade required writing and math. It also required transportation. Travel by land was difficult and took a long time. But Mesopotamians had another option. Closeness to the Tigris and the Euphrates Rivers meant they could travel by water. So, boats were invented!

People provided the power to move the earliest boats. It was easy traveling downstream, in the direction the river current flowed. But going upstream, against the current, was much harder. Eventually, sails were invented to take advantage of wind power.

The sails were simply squares of cloth. With modern sailboats, it's possible to change the positions of the sails to take advantage of changing wind directions. The Mesopotamians couldn't do that. Their sailboats could move only when the wind was blowing in the right direction.

THAT'S FASCINATING!

Early sailboats were used for fishing as well as trade.

THIS CYLINDER SEAL (RIGHT) AND ITS IMPRESSION (BELOW) SHOW A SEATED FIGURE WITH A LONG OAR MOVING AN EARLY MESOPOTAMIAN BOAT.

Taking a Risk

Mesopotamians didn't just sail and trade up and down the Tigris and the Euphrates Rivers. Eventually, they made it all the way to what is now the country of India. They sailed down what is today the Persian Gulf and across the Indian Ocean. That's a distance of around 1,780 miles (2,865 km)! That's an amazing and bold undertaking when you consider the simple boats they were using.

Medicine Beyond MAGIC

As you read earlier, Mesopotamians believed everything in the universe acted according to the gods' will. That might lead you to expect magic to be part of the practice of medicine in Mesopotamia. And it was. There was a kind of Mesopotamian doctor who relied on magic spells and amulets, which were charms meant to protect the wearer against disease.

But there was another type of doctor whose practice will sound familiar. This kind of doctor checked a patient's pulse and temperature, figured out the illness, and ordered a treatment. This doctor had pills and bandages, performed operations, and knew the importance of cleanliness and washing hands.

This second type of doctor could be a specialist. There were doctors for children and women. There were dentists and eye doctors. There were even veterinarians!

THAT'S FASCINATING!

Women and men could both be doctors in Mesopotamia. However, the reality was that women were rarely doctors.

THIS SCULPTURE IS BELIEVED TO SHOW GULA, THE MESOPOTAMIAN GODDESS OF HEALTH AND HEALING.

The Hand of the God

The second type of doctor seems almost modern. However, even this doctor viewed disease as the result of a sin the patient had committed, thus angering a god. In fact, in documents, diseases were usually not given a name such as the flu or a cold. Instead, the documents "named" a disease by saying "the hand of" a particular god or spirit touched the patient. The cure depended on the patient confessing their sin, accepting the proper treatment, and pleasing the god.

The Cradle of CIVILIZATION

Maybe you hadn't heard of Mesopotamia before this, but by now, it should be obvious why it's known as the Cradle of Civilization. It was a land of "firsts"—the first cities, the first writing, the first civilizations, and so many more.

The first schools, the first aquarium, and the first library catalog appeared in Mesopotamia. It was the first place to have a lawmaking body divided into two parts, or houses, like the U.S. Congress. It's where the first recorded love song and lullaby were written.

Mesopotamians invented the arch, an important development in architecture. They created the first maps. They invented musical instruments such as harps and lyres. They created the loom for making cloth. Developments in Mesopotamia changed the world forever.

THAT'S FASCINATING!

The collection of laws called the Code of Hammurabi was discovered in 1901. It's on display at the Louvre museum in Paris, France.

MESOPOTAMIAN CREATIONS

FARMING
IRRIGATION
PLOWS
RAISING ANIMALS
CITIES
SPECIALIZED TRADES
MONUMENTAL ARCHITECTURE
ARCHES
WHEELS
CHARIOTS
WRITING
COUNTING
MATHEMATICS
TIME MEASUREMENT
CALENDARS
ASTROLOGY
SAILBOATS
MEDICINE
SCHOOLS
AQUARIUMS
LIBRARY CATALOGS
TWO-PART LAWMAKING BODIES
LOVE SONGS
LULLABIES
MAPS
HARPS
LYRES
LOOMS
WINE AND BEER

Law Codes

Mesopotamia is also famous for its law codes. The best known of these is the Code of Hammurabi, which was written about 1750 BCE. Hammurabi was a Mesopotamian ruler, and his code was composed of the legal decisions he had made during his rule. It was carved on a stone stele and covers economic issues, family law, criminal law, and civil (or noncriminal) law. It shows his concerns for those who have little power in society, including widows and orphans.

GLOSSARY

architecture: the design of buildings

chariot: a carriage with two or four wheels that was pulled by horses

crescent: a curved shape, such as the moon when less than half of it is visible

document: a formal piece of writing

epic: describing a story about a hero

horoscope: advice and forecasts about events based on a person's birth date and the positions of the stars and planets

monumental: having a large size

nomadic: moving from place to place instead of living in one place all the time

pottery: objects such as bowls, plates, and vases that are made by hand out of clay and then baked at a high temperature so they become hard

stele: a carved stone slab used to mark important events

transportation: a way of traveling from one place to another

vehicle: an object used for carrying people or goods, such as a car, truck, or boat

zodiac: an imaginary area in the sky that the sun, moon, and planets appear to travel through. It's divided into 12 parts, which are associated with constellations and which some people believe determine people's character and fate.

FOR MORE INFORMATION

BOOKS

Nardo, Don. *Ancient Mesopotamia*. Lake Elmo, MN: Focus Readers, 2020.

Rodger, Ellen. *Ancient Mesopotamia Inside Out*. New York, NY: Crabtree Publishing, 2017.

WEBSITES

Ancient Mesopotamian Civilizations
www.khanacademy.org/humanities/world-history/world-history-beginnings/ancient-mesopotamia/a/mesopotamia-article
Learn more about ancient Mesopotamian civilizations on this website.

Ancient Mesopotamia 101
www.nationalgeographic.org/video/ancient-mesopotamia-101/
Watch a video about ancient Mesopotamia here.

Mesopotamia
www.mesopotamia.co.uk/index.html
Discover more about Mesopotamia on this interactive British Museum site.

Publisher's note to educators and parents: Our editors have carefully reviewed these websites to ensure that they are suitable for students. Many websites change frequently, however, and we cannot guarantee that a site's future contents will continue to meet our high standards of quality and educational value. Be advised that students should be closely supervised whenever they access the internet.

INDEX

agriculture/farming 5, 6, 7, 8, 9, 10, 29

architecture 12, 28, 29

art 10, 11, 15

astrology 22, 23, 29

boats/sailboats 24, 25, 29

calendar 22, 29

chariots 14, 15, 29

cities 4, 8, 9, 10, 12, 14, 15, 16, 18, 28, 29

city-states 9

Code of Hammurabi 28, 29

concrete 12

counting/numbers 18, 19, 21, 29

cuneiform 16, 17, 18, 19

cylinder seals 11, 25

Epic of Gilgamesh, The 17

Eridu 8

hunter-gatherers 6, 8

Jarmo 7, 8

law codes 28, 29

medicine/doctors 26, 27, 29

place value 18, 19

potter's wheel 14, 15

raising animals 6, 7, 29

time measurement 20, 21, 29

trade/trading 9, 16, 18, 24, 25

Ur 10, 12, 15

Uruk 8, 9, 12, 16, 17

wheel 4, 14, 29

Woolley, Leonard 15

writing 4, 16, 18, 24, 28, 29

ziggurats 12, 13